World Black History

African Roots

Melody Herr

Heinemann Library
Chicago, Illinois

www.heinemannraintree.com
Visit our website to find out
more information about
Heinemann-Raintree books.

To order:

☎ Phone 888-454-2279

💻 Visit www.heinemannraintree.com
to browse our catalog and order online.

©2010 Heinemann Library
an imprint of Capstone Global Library, LLC
Chicago, Illinois

Edited by David Andrews, Louise Galpine, and Abby Colich
Designed by Ryan Frieson and Betsy Wernert
Illustrated by Mapping Specialists
Picture research by Mica Brancic
Originated by Heinemann Library
Printed an bound in the United States of America,
North Mankato, MN

13 12 11
10 9 8 7 6 5 4 3 2

Library of Congress Cataloging-in-Publication Data
Herr, Melody.
    African roots / Melody Herr.
        p. cm. -- (World Black history)
    Includes bibliographical references and index.
    ISBN 978-1-4329-2383-9 (hc) -- ISBN 978-1-4329-2390-7
(pb) 1. Africa--History--Juvenile literature. 2. Africa--Kings
and rulers--Juvenile literature. 3. Africans--History--Juvenile
literature. I. Title.
    DT22.H396 2009
    960--dc22
                                    2009003231

102011
006373RP

Acknowledgments

The author and publishers are grateful to the following for
permission to reproduce copyright material: ©Alamy p. **14**
(The London Art Archive); ©The Bridgeman Art Library p.
32 (Private Collection/Photo ©Heini Schneebeli); ©Corbis
pp. **6** (Robert Harding World Imagery/©Nico Tondini),
7 (Kazuyoshi Nomachi), **8** (Remi Benali), **9**, **10** (George
Steinmetz), **11** (Smithsonian Institution), **12** (The Art
Archive/Alfredo Dagli Orti), **15** (zefa/©Gregor Schuster), **16**
(The Art Archive/Alfredo Dagli Orti), **17** (Gian Berto Vanni),
18 (Jonathan Blair), **20** (Bettmann), **23** (Gallo Images), **24**
(Dave Bartruff), **25** (Reuters/©Radu Sigheti), **31** (Godong/
©Michel Gounot), **33** (Charles & Josette Lenars), **35** (Yann
Arthus-Bertrand), **36** (JAI/©Gavin Hellier), **37** (The Gallery
Collection), **39** (Kazuyoshi Nomachi), **40** (Robert Holmes),
41 (Robert Holmes), **42** (Robert Harding World Imagery);
©Getty Images pp. **4** (Malcolm Linton), **21** (Mansell/Time
Life Pictures), **29** (Robert Harding World Imagery/Peter
Groenendijk); ©Hebrew University, Jerusalem p. **27** (Courtesy
of Historic Cities Research Project: historic-cities.huji.ac.il
The National Library of Israel , Shapell Family Digitization
Project, Eran Laor Cartographic Collection and The Hebrew
University of Jerusalem); ©Photolibrary pp. **19** (age fotostock/
Sylvain Grandadam), **43** (John Warburton-Lee Photography/
Nigel Pavitt); ©Shutterstock p. **28** (Tommy Ingberg);
©Smithsonian Institution p. **34** (Eliot Elisofon Photographic
Archives/National Museum of African Art).

Cover photograph of a young Dinka man standing on a
hillock amidst a herd of cattle at a settlement along Nile River
reproduced with permission of Panos/Sven Torfinn.

We would like to thank Marika Sherwood and Stephanie
Davenport for their invaluable help in the preparation of this
book.

Contents

Some words are shown in bold, **like this**. You can find out what they mean by looking in the Glossary.

The Many Lands of Africa

Sailors guide their boats to shore. Hunters stalk a rhinoceros. Traders ride camels through the sand. Farmers plant crops along the riverbank. Builders lay stones for a king's tomb. Wise men study holy books. All these scenes come from the history of Africa, a land of many diverse societies.

Mapping Africa

Africa is a huge continent, larger than North America and nearly three times the size of Europe. Africa has many different environments. Grasslands cover large areas of the continent, and a tropical rain forest lies in the middle. Africa also has vast deserts. The most famous is the world's largest desert, the Sahara.

In each of these areas, Africans developed unique ways of life, with their own religions, languages, governments, arts, and music.

Africa is home to many different societies, with different ways of life.

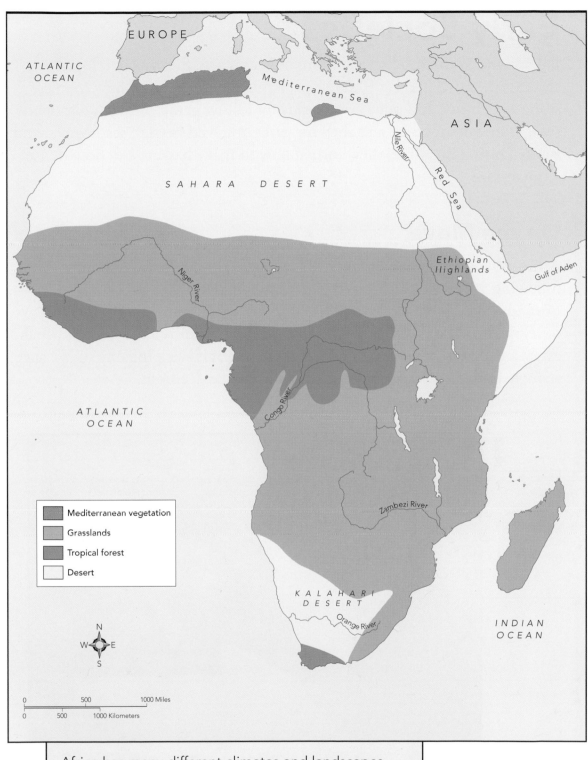

EUROPE

ATLANTIC
OCEAN

Mediterranean Sea

ASIA

SAHARA DESERT

Nile River

Red Sea

Niger River

Ethiopian
Highlands

Gulf of Aden

ATLANTIC
OCEAN

Congo River

Zambezi River

Mediterranean vegetation

Grasslands

Tropical forest

Desert

KALAHARI
DESERT

Orange River

INDIAN
OCEAN

N
W · E
S

| 0 | 500 | 1000 Miles |
| 0 | 500 | 1000 Kilometers |

Africa has many different climates and landscapes.

Early Societies

During the **Stone Age**, several thousand years ago, humans developed a successful way of life. By 10,000 BCE, African hunters knew how to make stone spearheads and bone arrowheads for killing **game**. Africans also made tools from wood, bone, and shell for gathering wild berries, seeds, nuts, and roots. During this time, they learned how to make baskets and how to use animal skins.

On the Move

Africans who depended on hunting and gathering moved constantly, following wild herds and looking for seasonal plants. These people, called **nomads**, lived in family groups of 20 to 50. Over time, as these groups developed rules for getting along, they became organized societies in which every person knew his or her role. A society of this size probably didn't have a single leader. Instead, everyone helped to make decisions.

Early humans shaped stones into tools, such as these axes used in northern Africa.

Rock Art

Rock paintings tell us about Stone Age Africans' tools, hunting methods, and religious ideas. Africans continued to make rock paintings long after the end of the Stone Age. Paintings done in the 1800s, for example, show battles between Africans and Europeans. Some African societies continue to paint on rocks today although they also make other forms of art.

Cave paintings such as these in the Sahara Desert give clues about the history of Africa.

Settled Societies

Africans who lived along lakes and rivers developed a different way of life. Instead of hunting big game, they fished with spears and nets. They also gathered edible reeds and other water plants. Because these people didn't need to move constantly in search of food, they built villages that grew into societies with as many as one thousand people.

Rules for Getting Along

With so many people living together, the villagers probably made rules for settling arguments, dividing the work, and choosing leaders. Although these rules may have been very simple, they marked the beginning of law and government.

Africans began herding cattle several thousand years ago.

First Herders

Over time, hunters who followed wild herds learned how to care for animals. They began to raise their own small herds. These new herders continued to live as nomads, moving from place to place as they searched for grass and water for their animals. Their herds provided them with a dependable supply of milk and meat.

The First Pets

Dogs were the first animals tamed by humans. According to an African legend, a dog and a man made a deal. The dog promised to help the man hunt in return for food and a warm place to sleep. Ever since, dogs and humans have been friends.

According to some historians, hunters living in North Africa began herding cattle, sheep, and goats around 5800 BCE. Herding began on the grasslands of eastern Africa around 3000 BCE. Rock paintings from this time show African herders with their animals.

First Farmers

Just as herders learned to raise wild animals, farmers learned to care for plants and save some of the seeds to plant again. Just as herders carefully chose which animals to breed, early farmers chose which seeds to plant each year. Over time, farmers developed new varieties of plants that were very different than the wild varieties.

Different Climates

The first African farmers lived in North Africa, near the Nile River, around 6000 BCE. They raised grains such as barley, **sorghum**, and **millet**. Around 3000 BCE, Africans on the grasslands of western and central Africa also began to raise sorghum and millet.

These grains didn't grow well in the tropical forests of central Africa, however. There, farmers grew yams, gourds, and palm trees. In the Ethiopian Highlands, farmers raised other crops, such as the cowpea, which were better suited to the environment.

African farmers planted barley, a type of grain.

How Do We Know?

There are no books from ancient times to tell us what life was like in Africa, so how can we know? **Archaeologists** fit together many clues, like pieces of a puzzle, to build a picture of early African societies.

Tools are important clues. Spearheads the size of a person's fist suggest that hunters stalked zebras and other big game. Arrowheads the size of a miniature candy bar suggest they hunted birds and other small animals. Long knives and grinding stones show that Africans cut grasses and pounded the seeds to make flour.

By collecting pollen samples, archaeologists learn about the environment in prehistoric times. By studying the size and layout of a village, they figure out how many people lived there and how they organized their society.

Many pieces of the puzzle are missing, and science isn't the only source of information. Africans have many ways of preserving their history, from art and music to traditional stories.

Archaeologists excavate ruins from the ancient kingdom of Axum in present-day Ethiopia.

Herding and Farming

Some African societies combined herding and agriculture. Farmers in the Ethiopian Highlands, for example, raised both crops and cattle. This combination provided a healthy diet of milk, meat, grains, and vegetables.

Although they chose different ways of life, herders and farmers traded with one another for meat, grain, and animal skins. Their trade network included the Africans who, instead of switching to herding or agriculture, chose to continue hunting and gathering.

Changing Societies

The development of agriculture led to a whole new way of life. Farmers settled in villages. They invented new tools for planting and harvesting the crops. They also made pottery for storing and cooking food. Over time, the **population** grew. In order to keep so many people living and working together peacefully, settled agricultural societies invented new forms of law and government.

This statue shows an early leader from the kingdom of Benin.

Egypt and the Nile River

The Nile River valley in northeast Africa was one of the first places where Africans switched from hunting and gathering to agriculture. Crops grew well on the fertile land, and farmers raised wheat, barley, fruits, and vegetables. Farmers also kept cattle, sheep, goats, ducks, and geese. Fish, antelope, and wild birds provided meat as well. Thanks to this plentiful food supply, the **population** grew and villages became cities. The first city in Africa, Hierakonpolis, appeared before 3500 BCE.

Hierakonpolis became the center of the kingdom of Upper Egypt. Around 3200 BCE, the ruler of Upper Egypt, King Menes, united his kingdom and the kingdom of Lower Egypt. Ruling this vast double kingdom, which stretched along the Nile from the highlands to the sea, required a new form of government.

This plaque pictures the rulers of Upper and Lower Egypt. The animals with knotted necks symbolize the union of the two kingdoms.

The Nile River

The Nile is the world's longest river, measuring 6,650 kilometers (4,132 miles). Without the Nile, Egypt would have been a desert. Every year the river floods from July through October. Then the river goes back down, leaving behind a layer of black mud that fertilizes the land.

The Blue Nile and the Atbara River, two of the Nile's major **tributaries**, begin in the Ethiopian Highlands. The third tributary, the White Nile, begins in the lakes of eastern Africa. Swelling with water from these three rivers, the great Nile flows into the Mediterranean Sea.

Traveling the Nile

Egyptians used the Nile as a water highway. To go north, boatmen simply rode the **current**. To go south, they put up sails to catch the wind. Unfortunately, a boat couldn't travel the Nile's entire length because of a series of six waterfalls, called **cataracts**.

The Nile River helped Egypt become a prosperous kingdom.

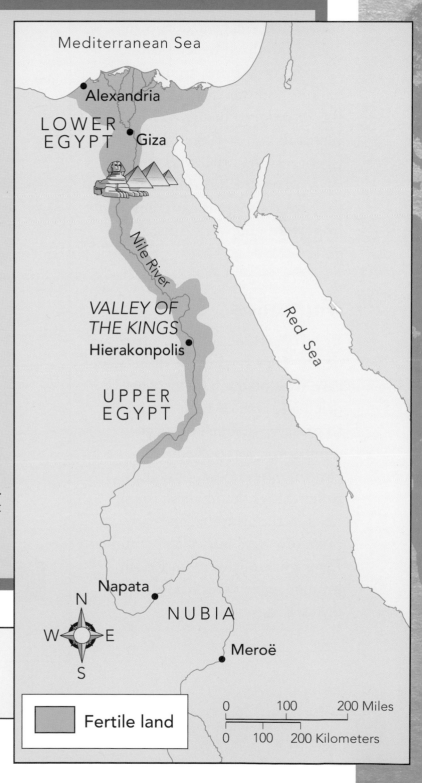

Mediterranean Sea

Alexandria

LOWER EGYPT

Giza

Nile River

VALLEY OF THE KINGS

Hierakonpolis

UPPER EGYPT

Red Sea

Napata

NUBIA

N
W E
S

Meroë

Fertile land

0   100   200 Miles

0   100   200 Kilometers

Egyptian Religion

The Egyptians worshiped many gods. Each village had its own god, symbolized by a crocodile, a beetle, or another animal. The highest god was the sun god Ra. In order to justify their rule, **pharaohs**, the rulers of ancient Egypt, claimed that they were descendants of Ra, and that they were also gods. Another important god was Osiris, the god of the dead.

Mummies

Egyptians believed in life after death. They treated the dead with care. The pharaoh's body was dried and treated with chemicals to preserve it. The body, called a **mummy**, was buried with clothing, food, weapons, and other things the pharaoh might need in the afterlife. The early pharaohs were buried in pyramids. Later pharaohs were buried in human-made caves in the Valley of the Kings.

Egyptians worshiped the cat goddess, Bastet, who was sometimes pictured as a cat with the body of a woman.

Egyptian Society

Egyptians organized their society like a pyramid. The pharaoh was at the top, priests and government officials were in the middle, and **peasant** farmers were at the bottom. Every year, peasants paid taxes with a share of their crops. Officials decided how much tax to collect by measuring the water level of the Nile, which determined the size of the harvest.

Egyptian Science

Egyptians made many discoveries in science and technology. Mathematicians used geometry to build the pyramids and to measure the land along the Nile. Inventors made a water clock to keep time and an instrument to record the water level of the Nile. **Astronomers** who studied the stars created a calendar to predict when the Nile would flood.

Writing in Egypt

Egyptians used a system of writing called **hieroglyphics**. This system used symbols instead of letters. Some symbols were pictures of real things. Other symbols stood for word sounds. Officials wrote government records and letters on a kind of paper called **papyrus**.

Egyptian writing used pictures instead of an alphabet.

Rulers of North Africa

Other kings envied Egypt's wealth. So they decided to claim it for themselves. After 800 BCE, several new rulers conquered Egypt and other parts of North Africa.

Nile Neighbors

Egyptian traders traveled up the Nile to the region of Nubia (in present-day Sudan), where they bought gold and stone for building. (See the map on page 13.) Around 1500 BCE, the Egyptian **pharaohs** sent armies to conquer Nubia and put their own officials in charge. For the next 500 years, while Egypt ruled Nubia, the Nubians adopted Egyptian language and religion.

Around 1000 BCE, the Nubians began to build their own kingdom, called Kush. As Kush grew strong, it broke away from Egypt. In 730 BCE, the Nubian leader Piye attacked Egypt and declared himself the new pharaoh. After his victory, however, Piye went home to Nubia. A few years later, his brother and successor, Shabaka, came to rule Egypt.

Egyptian artists portrayed two Nubians in the 1100s BCE.

Taharqa, the Nubian Pharaoh

The most famous Nubian pharaoh was Taharqa. Crowned in 690 BCE, he ruled the double kingdom of Nubia and Egypt for 26 years.

Taharqa built many monuments. In Napata, the Nubian capital, he built two temples. Then he had his name carved on the peak of the holy mountain Jebel Barkal and covered his name with gold. Taharqa also built new additions to the sun god's temple. He ordered artists to carve gigantic statues of himself and his mother. Throughout his kingdom, he placed more statues of himself and symbols of his name. Finally, he built a pyramid for his tomb.

Taharqa was the last Nubian pharaoh. In 664 BCE, the Assyrian army from the **Middle East** conquered Egypt. Taharqa fled back to Nubia.

The pharoah Taharqa ordered many artists to carve giant statues of himself. On many of them, his nose is missing and his royal crown is broken. Some historians say his enemies destroyed the statues.

Rulers of Meroë built pyramids similar to the Egyptian pyramids.

Meroë, the Great City

When the Assyrians invaded, the Nubian pharaohs left Egypt. Around 550 BCE, they moved farther south and built the city of Meroë.

The Nubians chose a good place for their capital city. Meroë stood close to two water highways, the Nile River and the Red Sea. Merchants came from distant lands to trade gold, ivory, ostrich feathers, leopard skins, and other luxuries. In addition, the land around Meroë was good for agriculture. Farmers raised crops and cattle.

Early Ironwork

Meroë also had an important natural resource: iron **ore**. Iron was stronger and easier to shape than stone, copper, or bronze. It also made better tools for farming and better weapons for hunting and fighting. Meroë became one of the first iron-working societies in Africa. Iron technology was key to its success.

Nubian Society

In Nubia, as in Egypt, **peasant** farmers were in the lowest class of citizens. Next came priests, nobles, and officials. At the top stood a powerful king or queen.

Nubian rulers relied on taxes and income from foreign trade to run the government. At first, officials used Egyptian **hieroglyphics** to keep records, but eventually they developed their own writing system.

Rulers also used their wealth to build pyramids. Nubian pyramids are shorter and have steeper sides than Egyptian pyramids. They are made of smaller blocks. Also, Egyptian pharaohs were buried inside pyramids, but Nubian rulers were buried underneath pyramids, in tombs cut into the rock.

The Nubian kingdom, with the capital at Meroë, lasted from about 550 BCE until about 350 CE.

The Lion God

The Nubians worshiped many gods, such as the lion god Apedemek. Apedemek was a war god, but he also stood for wisdom. Artists portrayed him as a snake or a man with a lion's head.

The god Apedemek was part human and part animal.

Greek Pharaohs

While the Nubians were creating a new society in Meroë, Egypt came under another set of rulers. In 332 BCE, the Greeks came from their small nation across the Mediterranean Sea and conquered Egypt. Greek-speaking pharaohs ruled Egypt for the next 300 years.

Instead of replacing Egyptian society, the new pharaohs mixed Greek and Egyptian ways of life. They hired Egyptians as government officials, for example, and taught them the Greek language and alphabet.

Mediterranean Trade

Although agriculture remained important, the Greek-speaking pharaohs extended the long-established cross-Mediterranean trade. Soon Egypt had nearly 4,000 ships to carry grain, medicine, cloth, jewelry, and wild animals to cities around the Mediterranean. Egyptians also traded ivory, gems, and spices with merchants from other parts of Africa, India, and Arabia.

The Library at Alexandria

The Greek pharaohs built the city of Alexandria as a trade port, but it became a center for learning as well. At the library and museum, scholars studied literature, science, medicine, mathematics, and geography.

Scholars from distant lands visited the library at Alexandria.

This carving shows Roman soldiers who conquered and ruled Africa in 30 BCE.

Roman Conquest

In 30 BCE, Egypt was conquered again, this time by the Romans. The Romans came from present-day Italy. They ruled a huge empire covering the lands around the Mediterranean Sea. They wanted to rule Africa, too, because it had good farmland that they needed to produce wheat and olive oil. The Romans first conquered the city of Carthage in 146 BCE. Then they slowly spread across North Africa. The conquest of Egypt was one of their last great victories in Africa.

Strict Rule

The Romans were harsh rulers. They taxed the peasants so much that some gave up farming. Meanwhile, the wealthy set up grand estates where enslaved men and women worked in the fields and olive orchards.

At last, around 400 CE, as a result of a failing government and attacks from foreign armies, the Roman Empire fell apart and the Romans left Africa.

Kingdom in the Highlands

On a high plateau east of the Nile, another kingdom, called Axum, rose to power. Beginning in the first century CE, the trade network across the Red Sea helped this small kingdom grow wealthy. Around 350 CE, King Ezana began to expand this kingdom. With his army, he first conquered the Nubian city of Meroë. Then he continued fighting wars against other kings until his empire covered the area that is now Ethiopia and the Sudan.

Axum Grows

Over time, the kings who ruled Axum crossed the Red Sea and conquered the southern corner of Arabia. In order to rule their huge empire, they divided it into smaller areas. They relied on government officials in each of these **provinces** to collect taxes from local leaders and farmers.

The kings lived in Axum, the capital. Located in the highlands, Axum was a busy city of about 20,000 people.

Axum began as a small city but grew into a large kingdom.

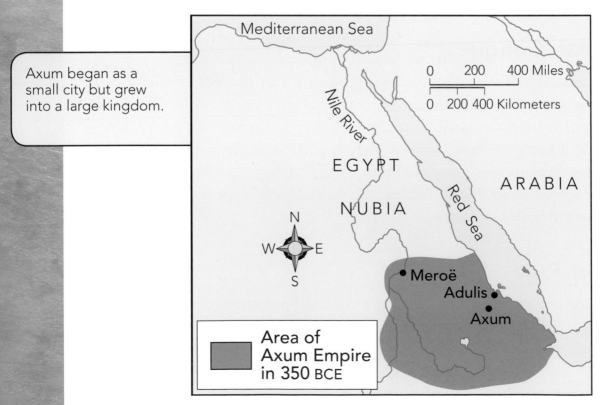

Leading City

The most important city in the kingdom of Axum was Adulis, located on the Red Sea. There, traders loaded gold, ivory, slaves, tortoise shells, and live elephants onto ships from Asia, the **Middle East**, and the Mediterranean lands. In the markets, merchants sold jewelry, silk, and other luxuries. The kings controlled the trade system and grew rich by taxing exports and imports.

Science and Technology

The citizens of Axum put science and technology to work. Government officials invented a new form of writing. Builders and architects constructed amazing stone monuments. At the same time, Axum farmers cut the hilly land into flat **terraces** and built an irrigation system to water the fields.

Axum Tombstones

These stones, called **stelae**, stand over the tombs of early Axum kings. The largest one still standing is a block of granite 25 meters (82 feet) tall. Builders hauled it here from a quarry more than 3.2 kilometers (2 miles) away.

Artists decorated stelae with beautiful carvings. These stones stand over the tombs of early Axum kings.

Religion in Axum

The people of Axum worshiped many gods. Some were their own gods, such as the war god Mahrem. Some were Greek gods, such as Poseidon, god of the sea.

A New Religion

King Ezana was the first African king to convert to Christianity and make it the official religion of his kingdom. Christianity was founded in the Middle East in the first century CE by the followers of Jesus of Nazareth. After his death, Jesus' followers began to spread his teachings to the rest of the world.

Christianity demanded the worship of only one god. For this reason, when King Ezana converted to Christianity, he forbade builders to put up monuments to other gods. Long after King Ezana's death, Christianity remained the leading religion in the highlands of Africa.

Paintings of Jesus appear in this Ethiopian Bible, the book that contains the teachings of Christianity.

Christianity in Africa

Over time, the leaders of Christianity in Europe created an official church, with a set of rules and beliefs. African Christians, however, had their own doctrines and their own churches. In northwest Africa, Berber societies mixed Christianity with their traditional religious beliefs and ceremonies. Meanwhile, in Egypt, some Africans interpreted Christian doctrines differently than the European church leaders did. These Africans developed another form of Christianity.

Christianity remained a minor religion in Africa, except in the eastern highlands and a few parts of North Africa. Then, after 1500 CE, European traders, colonists, and missionaries spread Christian teachings across Africa.

A Dream of Churches

King Lalibela ruled Ethiopia, a kingdom in the highlands, in the early 1200s CE. According to a legend, he dreamed that he was supposed to build churches. He awoke, and with the help of angels working at night, speedily built the churches. In fact, Christians built several churches during his reign.

St. George's Church was carved into rock in the early 1200s CE in Ethiopia.

Trade Cities in East Africa

Between 650 and 1400 CE, Africans living on the east coast, along the Indian Ocean, built a string of cities. The ocean served as a highway, connecting the cities with one another as well as with the **Middle East** and Asia. Over time, the citizens blended African traditions with new ideas from other parts of the world. This led them to create something new—Swahili society and language.

Sailing the Indian Ocean

Ship captains had to plan their voyages across the Indian Ocean carefully because ships depended on the power of the wind. When a captain from Asia or Arabia wanted to sail to Africa, he had to make the trip between November and February, while the wind was blowing west. He couldn't sail home until April, when the wind changed direction and blew east, toward Arabia and Asia.

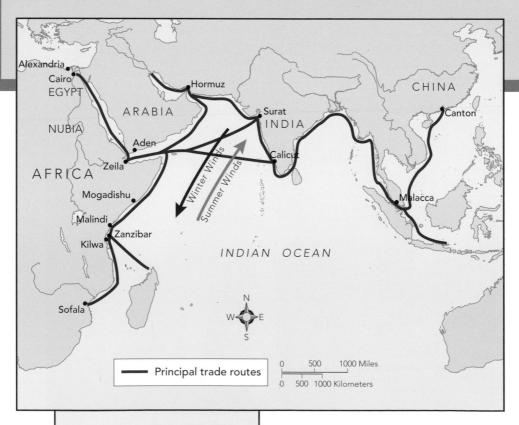

Trade routes linked Asia, Arabia, and Africa.

Swahili Trade Centers

The Swahili cities along the coast became famous trade centers, where traders from distant lands came to do business. Traders came from African villages hundreds of miles from the Indian Ocean with gold, copper, spices, and leopard skins to sell in the cities. They also sold elephant tusks, used for their ivory. Traders from the Middle East and Asia came to buy these products. In exchange, they sold silk, pottery, and cotton cloth. Meanwhile, traders sailing up and down the African coast carried all these things from one Swahili city to another.

Island City

One of the most famous cities in East Africa was Kilwa. Built on an island near the coast, the city had a good port. Travelers praised Kilwa for its gardens, orchards, and beautiful buildings. For example, one traveler who visited Kilwa in 1331 praised the wonderful fish, lemons, mangoes, and other foods he ate there.

In Kilwa merchants sold goods from Africa, Asia, and the Middle East.

QVILOA

Africans and Arabs

Around 650 CE, traders from Arabia, an area in the Middle East, began to settle in the coastal cities of East Africa. Together, Africans and Arabs invented a new language called Swahili. It was basically an African language with many borrowed Arabic words, and it was written in Arabic letters. In the same way, Africans and Arabs blended traditions and ideas to create Swahili society.

Social Classes

Swahili society was divided into classes. Enslaved Africans were at the bottom. Free African craftsmen, clerks, and other skilled workers came next. Merchants belonged to the upper class. The city's ruler and his family stood at the very top of society.

A New Fruit Arrives

Sailors from Indonesia, a group of islands in the Indian Ocean, brought the first bananas to Africa. Bananas grew well in the tropical climate, and African farmers quickly made bananas one of their main crops. Over time, they developed new varieties of bananas.

Sailors from Indonesia brought bananas to Africa where they became one of the main crops.

This photo shows the Great Mosque of Kilwa, built in the 1100s. It is one of the earliest remaining mosques on the East African coast.

Islam, A New Religion

In Swahili society, a person's ancestry determined his or her class. Arabic families had more prestige than African families. But Africans could rise on the social ladder by converting to the Arabic religion, Islam. Muhammad, an Arab trader who became a prophet, founded Islam around 620 CE. When he died in 632 CE, his followers, called **Muslims**, spread Islam to other parts of the world.

Islam Comes to Africa

Islam spread throughout East Africa. Arab traders who did business or settled in the Swahili cites brought their religion with them. Muslim holy men came to tell Africans about Islam.

As Islam spread throughout Africa, so did Arabic learning. Over time, some Africans adopted Arabic writing, science, math, and law to help them trade, run their governments, and build their societies.

The Kingdom of Ghana

West Africa had a rich history between 300 and 1500 CE—a history of warriors, traders, and kings. During this time, several kingdoms rose to power then fell into decline.

One of the first kingdoms was Ghana. (This kingdom was in a different area than today's nation of Ghana.) The Soninke people founded Ghana between the Senegal River and the Niger River around 300 CE. Although the land was good, trade was as important as farming.

Trade Routes

A number of trails crisscrossing the Sahara Desert linked Ghana to the Mediterranean Sea. Over these routes, traders carried gold and ivory to the coast. They brought back horses, salt, spices, silk, books, and metal tools and weapons.

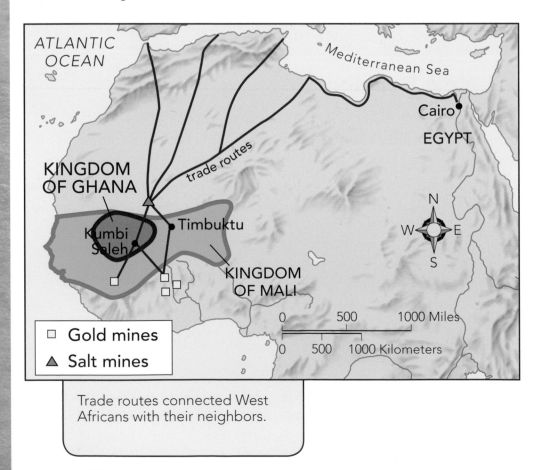

Trade routes connected West Africans with their neighbors.

Traders used camels to cross the desert. Camels could carry larger loads and travel farther than other animals.

A Desert Journey

The long, difficult journey across the Sahara could take as long as four months. In 1352 CE an Arab named Ibn Battuta wrote about his trip from North Africa to West Africa.

Ibn Battuta traveled with a **caravan** of traders. Traders traveled together because the desert was a dangerous place. Sometimes the sand blew so hard that the trail disappeared. In fact, one of the travelers got lost in the desert. Sometimes the traders walked for more than three weeks before they reached an **oasis** where they could fill their water bags and rest. Ibn Battuta was glad when his journey finally ended.

Why Use Camels?

Camels were known as the "ships of the desert." They originally came from the **Middle East**, but around 300 CE traders began to use them to cross the Sahara. Camels were far better than donkeys or horses for desert travel. They carried larger loads, endured the heat better, and walked farther without water.

Wealthy Kings

Ghana's kings grew wealthy by collecting taxes on trade goods. The kings dressed in expensive clothes and jewelry to show off their riches. They lived in a palace in the capital city, Kumbi Saleh. The kings also used their wealth to buy weapons and horses. As Ghana's armies conquered more and more territory, the empire grew.

Islam in Ghana

In addition to luxuries, trade brought Ghana new ideas, particularly Islam and Arabic learning. The kings did not convert to Islam. Instead, they continued to practice their traditional West African religion. But they allowed **Muslims** to live peacefully outside the capital city, in a separate town. The kings of Ghana also hired educated Muslims as government officials to keep records, write letters, and run the empire.

The Kingdom Falls

Ghana reached its peak around 1000 CE, but then it began to decline. A drought struck, crops died, and farmers couldn't produce enough food. Officials in the cities and towns of Ghana resisted the kings. At the same time, enemy armies attacked the empire, conquered the trade centers, and took over the trade routes. Though it was once a powerful kingdom, Ghana fell into ruins.

When drought strikes, it can leave villages in ruins and rivers dried up, such as the one below.

Revenge of the Black Snake

Archaeologists and historians say that drought and war caused Ghana's decline. Africans, however, have a legend that explains the fall of this ancient kingdom. Every year, Bida the black snake promised to give the people wealth if they sacrificed a young girl to him. But one year, a man named Mamdou Sarolle saved the girl promised to Bida because he loved her and wanted to marry her. Angrily, Bida took revenge and made the crops dry up.

Powerful Kings of Mali

Sundiata the warrior-king founded the kingdom of Mali. His people, the Malinke, lived along the Niger River. Their land was under the control of Sumanguru, the last king of ancient Ghana.

Sundiata the Hero

The Malinke leaders came to Sundiata and asked him to drive out their enemies. He agreed. By uniting all the Malinke armies, he defeated Sumanguru in 1235 CE at the Battle of Kirina. As a result of this victory, Sundiata became the highest king of the new Mali kingdom.

Sundiata made the city of Niani his capital. Then he went on to conquer the gold mines and the key cities so that Mali could control the Sahara trade system. He even conquered Ghana's capital, Kumbi Saleh.

African storytellers tell many legends about the warrior-king Sundiata and his adventures. This sculpture illustrates a scene from one of those legends.

The Mali kingdom rose up along the Niger River.

Mali Grows

After Sundiata's death, around 1255 CE, the Mali kingdom continued to grow. By 1300 CE it was bigger and more powerful than Ghana had been. Mali stretched from the Atlantic coast into central Africa and from the edge of the Sahara Desert to the Bure gold mines. (See the map on page 30.) Trade in gold and salt made Mali wealthy, but it wasn't the only reason for Mali's success. Fertile land also helped Mali prosper. Farmers raised crops along the Niger River, while herders raised cattle on the grassland. With plenty of food, the **population** grew.

Valuable Snail Shells

In the kingdom of Mali, traders used cowrie shells as money. The cowrie is a sea snail that lives on the other side of Africa, in the Indian Ocean (as well as the Pacific Ocean). One kind of cowrie grows to 10 centimeters (4 inches) long. Pacific islanders wear these shells as jewelry. The cowrie used for money is only 2.5 centimeters (1 inch) long.

Government in Mali

A strong, well-organized government made Mali powerful. The king appointed officials for specific duties, such as collecting taxes or managing farmland. He also appointed his relatives and other loyal men to rule the towns far from Niani, the capital.

Islam in Mali

Although some citizens of Mali continued to practice traditional African religions, others converted to Islam. When Ibn Battuta visited Mali in 1352, he noticed how devout the **Muslims** were:

> They are careful to observe the hours of prayer, and **assiduous** in attending them in **congregations**, and in bringing up their children to them. On Fridays [the Islamic **sabbath**], if a man does not go early to the mosque, he cannot find a corner to pray in, on account of the crowd.... Even if a man has nothing but an old worn shirt, he washes it and cleans it, and wears it to the Friday service.

In West Africa, Muslims built mosques such as this one.

A Famous Muslim Ruler

The Mali king Mansa Musa was a Muslim. In 1324 he made a pilgrimage to Mecca, Islam's holy city in Arabia. On the way, he visited Cairo in Egypt and other cities. He showed off his wealth and gave many gifts in order to make friends with Muslim rulers in North Africa and the **Middle East**. He was said to be the richest man to ever visit Cairo.

When Mansa Musa returned from his pilgrimage, he brought to Mali architects to build mosques, scholars to advise him, and teachers to educate the citizens. He also started a famous university in the city of Timbuktu.

Mali's Decline

Mali began to decline in the early 1400s. The royal family argued over who should become the next king. Enemy armies attacked the kingdom. Timbuktu was captured. Meanwhile, Mali's **provinces** broke away from the empire. Mali, the great kingdom, fell apart.

Mansa Musa, shown in this illustration, helped build the university that made Timbuktu the center of learning in West Africa. Science, astronomy, mathematics, law, and theology, as well as many other subjects, were taught there.

Great Zimbabwe

Around 1100 CE, Africans in the Southeast built the city of Great Zimbabwe. For more than 1,000 years, they had been farmers on the grasslands. Gradually, they became traders as well.

Well-Ordered Society

Since about 100 CE, these farmers had lived in villages of 50 to 400 people, where each person knew his or her place. A married man had authority over his wives and children. His family lived in a cluster of huts, made of stone, mud bricks, or wood, with thatched roofs. Each wife had her own hut. The unmarried men shared one hut, while the unmarried women shared another.

Men and women divided the work. Men herded cattle and hunted **game**. Women raised the crops and did the cooking. When there was enough rain, the villagers had a good diet of vegetables, milk, and meat. But during a drought, the crops failed and hunger struck.

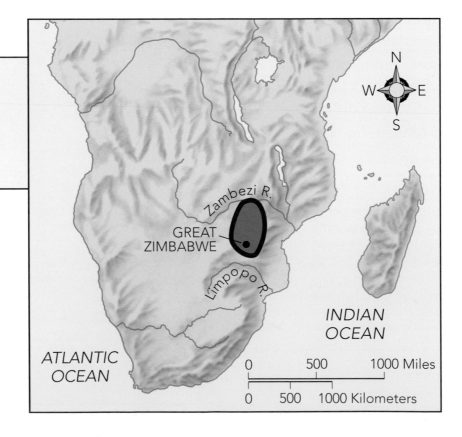

Great Zimbabwe was in southern Africa, in the present-day country of Zimbabwe.

Cattle and Riches

Cattle were a form of wealth in southeast Africa. When a man wanted to get married, he gave the bride's family cattle. When a chief settled an argument, the villagers paid him with cattle.

Cattle are still a source of wealth in Africa today.

The Role of the Chief

A chief would rule all the villages in his territory, which might include 1,000 to 50,000 people. With the help of his relatives and advisers, he settled arguments and made decisions.

Every few years, the chief gathered the teenage boys for schooling. Older men taught them traditions and all the skills they would need as adults. After this training, the boys were treated as grown men.

Iron and Gold

The land was rich in metal: iron, copper, tin, and gold. The **ore** was easy to mine because it lay near the surface instead of deep in the ground. Blacksmiths made iron hoes, knives, weapons, and tools. They also made copper jewelry.

Trade in Southern Africa

Villagers living on the grasslands near ore deposits traded with villagers living near the coast who didn't have these metals. Over time, as trade became more important, societies in southeast Africa changed. The **population** grew and cities sprang up. Rulers became richer and more powerful.

Great Zimbabwe

Great Zimbabwe became one of the new trading cities. Built between 1100 and 1400 CE, it stood on the grassland between the Zambezi River and the Limpopo River. (This area is now in the modern nation of Zimbabwe.) The city spread over a large area, and as many as 20,000 people lived there.

The Great Enclosure

The heart of Great Zimbabwe was the Great Enclosure. Its outer wall was 250 meters (820 feet) around and 11 meters (36 feet) at the highest point. Masons stacked the granite blocks so precisely that they didn't need to put mortar in the spaces between the stones.

The wall that protected the center of Great Zimbabwe still stands today.

A Wealthy Society

The people of Great Zimbabwe continued to farm and raise cattle, but their wealth depended on trade. They sold ivory, copper, iron, and gold to traders from the **Middle East**, Asia, and the Swahili cities to the north. With their profits, the traders of Great Zimbabwe bought ceramics from Asia, glass from Arabia, and other imported luxuries.

Decline

Sometime in the 1400s CE, the city of Great Zimbabwe was abandoned. Why? Today, **archaeologists** do not know the reasons why the people left, but many believe that the land could no longer support the huge population. Over time, farmers had worn out the soil and herders had let their cattle overgraze the grass. Finally, the families who lived in Great Zimbabwe had to move away and find new homes.

These carved figures, found at the ruins of Great Zimbabwe, may have had religious meaning.

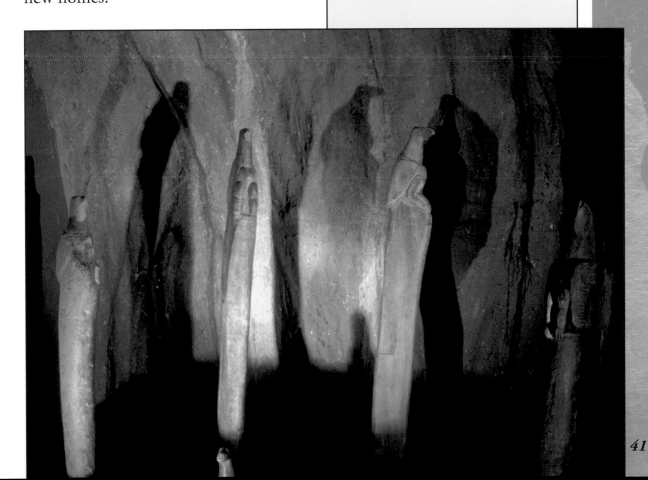

41

Claiming Africa's Past

Today, Great Zimbabwe is a symbol of Africans' achievements. The government of the present-day country of Zimbabwe made it a national monument. Its picture is stamped on the one dollar coin. In addition, in 1986 the United Nations recognized the importance of Great Zimbabwe and declared it a World Heritage Site. Great Zimbabwe belongs to all Africans and all people who trace their roots to Africa.

A Mysterious Tower

Inside the Great Enclosure, a narrow passage between the outer wall and an inner wall leads to this strange, cone-shaped tower. The tower is 10 meters (33 feet) high and 5 meters (16 feet) wide at its base. Did farmers use it as a silo to store grain? Did it have a religious purpose? **Archaeologists** are still trying to solve this mystery.

The ruins of the tower of Great Zimbabwe still stand today. Archaeologists are not sure what it was used for.

Visiting the Past

Today tourists can visit the Nubian pyramids and the tombs of Egyptian **pharaohs**. In East Africa, they can tour the Christian churches carved into rock or walk through the Swahili cities along the coast. If they go to West Africa, they can see the mosques built by Mansa Musa. These places are reminders of ancient African societies.

Many Mysteries

Archaeologists have not yet solved all the mysteries about how the people of these societies lived. At the same time, there are many other ancient African societies that archaeologists may never discover because all the remains have disappeared. Sometimes the only clues about these societies are Africans' oral traditions—stories about history passed on from person to person for thousands of years.

Every year, we learn more about Africa in ancient times and Africans' many great achievements.

These women in Namibia participate in traditional song and dance.

Timeline

40,000–10,000 BCE

Africans use stone tools and live by hunting and gathering.

9000–3000 BCE

Africans discover how to raise plants and tame animals.

3500 BCE

The first known city in Africa, Hierakonpolis, appears.

3200 BCE

King Menes unites Upper and Lower Egypt.

3200–2755 BCE

Egyptians invent **hieroglyphics**.

2755–2255 BCE

Egyptians build the first pyramids.

1500 BCE

Egyptian rulers conquer Nubia.

950 BCE

Nubia wins independence.

730 BCE

Nubian rulers conquer Egypt.

690 BCE

Taharqa becomes **pharaoh** of the double kingdom of Nubia and Egypt.

664 BCE

The Assyrian army drives the Nubians out of Egypt.

553 BCE

Nubian rulers make Meroë their capital.

332 BCE

The Greeks conquer Egypt.

30 BCE

The Romans conquer Egypt.

30 CE

Jesus of Nazareth and his followers start a new religion, Christianity.

50

Missionaries, traders, and refugees begin to bring Christianity to North Africa.

300

Traders use camels on the trans-Sahara trade route. The Soninke people begin building the kingdom of Ghana.

340

King Ezana of Axum attacks Meroë.

400

The Roman Empire falters and Romans leave Africa.

622

Muhammad and his followers start a new religion, Islam.

650

Arab traders begin to settle on the East Coast of Africa.

800

Ghana becomes a powerful kingdom.

1100

Shona-speaking people begin to build Great Zimbabwe.

1150

The Swahili city-states become important trade centers.

1235

Sundiata founds the kingdom of Mali.

1324

Mansa Musa, the ruler of Mali, makes a pilgrimage to the Islamic holy city of Mecca.

1400s

Great Zimbabwe is abandoned.

Glossary

archaeologist a scientist who studies societies of the past

assiduous constant or faithful

astronomer a scientist who studies the sun, moon, stars, and planets

caravan a group of people traveling together

cataract a set of small waterfalls in a river

congregation a gathering of people, usually for religious worship

current the flow of a river or an ocean in one direction

game wild animals that are hunted

hieroglyphics a form of writing using pictures

Middle East area of land between Africa and Asia

millet a type of grain

mummy a dried, preserved body

Muslim a person who practices the religion Islam

nomad a person who moves from place to place

oasis a place in the desert where water is available

ore raw minerals from which metal is removed

papyrus an early type of paper

peasant a person who lives in a rural area; a farmworker

pharaoh the title for the ruler of Egypt and Nubia

population a group of persons living in the same place

province a small part of a kingdom or an empire

sabbath a day of the week reserved for religious observances

sorghum a type of grain

stelae stone pillars, usually with words or pictures carved on them

Stone Age period when humans made tools from stone

terrace a level piece of ground cut into the side of a hill so that it can be farmed

tributary a river that flows into a larger river or a lake

Find Out More

Books

Barr, Gary E. *History and Activities of the West African Kingdoms*. Chicago: Heinemann Library, 2007.

Bowden, Rob, and Rosie Wilson. *Ancient Africa*. Chicago: Heinemann Library, 2009.

Richardson, Hazel. *Life in Ancient Africa*. New York: Crabtree, 2005.

Schomp, Virgina. *The Ancient Africans*. New York: Marshall Cavendish Benchmark, 2008.

Sherrow, Victoria. *Ancient Africa: Archaeology Unlocks the Secrets of Africa's Past*. Washington, DC: National Geographic Society, 2007.

Websites

Africa for Kids
http://africa.mrdonn.org/index.html

BBC World Service, The Story of Africa
http://www.bbc.co.uk/worldservice/specials/1624_story_of_africa/

Civilizations in Africa
http://www.wsu.edu/%7Edee/CIVAFRCA/CIVAFRCA.HTM

Early African History for Kids
http://www.historyforkids.org/learn/africa/history/index.htm

Mali Empire and Djenne Figures
http://africa.si.edu/exhibits/resources/mali/index.htm

Index